ZION NATIONAL PARK

A SCENIC WONDERLAND

BY STEVEN L. WALKER

Above: Towering cottonwoods frame a waterfall at the Temple of Sinawava in Zion Canyon on an afternoon in May at Zion National Park.
PHOTO BY JEFF GNASS

Left: Fremont cottonwoods, *Populus fremontii*, show the delicate green of early spring as they are backlit by the sun and stand in contrast to the Navajo sandstone walls of Zion Canyon.
PHOTO BY TERRY DONNELLY

Front cover: The Virgin River flowing beneath pinnacles of sandstone on an afternoon in late autumn. The Virgin River, one of the many tributaries of the Colorado River, is responsible for carving Zion Canyon.
PHOTO BY JEFF GNASS

5. Introduction

The massive monoliths of Zion Canyon, the delicate beauty of hanging gardens, desert varnish streaked sandstone walls, the colors of hardwoods through the seasons and mild climate create an environment as tranquil and inspiring as any on earth.

8. Geography

Zion National Park is northeast of St. George, in southwestern Utah, 320 miles south of Salt Lake City, Utah and 158 miles northeast of Las Vegas, Nevada. Remote location was responsible for late settlement by Europeans. It was not until 1858 that the first Mormon missionary explored the area in search of potential sites for suitable land for Mormon towns.

11. Geology

Volcanic activity, faulting, wind and water created the intricate layers of rock found in Zion. Nine different formations can be seen in the rocks of the region, each a history of its time, and forces of nature present, as it was laid.

17. Creation of the Canyon

The Virgin River, at times placid and others roiling, carved Zion Canyon through the layers of rock that form the canyon walls, in a process continuing today.

20. Wildlife

Zion National Park's unique landscape, with its shaded canyon walls, hanging gardens and riparian communities supports a variety of wildlife from Upper and Lower Sonoran, Transition and Canadian lifezones.

23. Flora

Zion National Park features an interesting variety of plant communities, a result of varying elevations, access to water and exposure to the sun.

26. The Festival of Fall

Hardwoods in Zion Canyon are always an inspiring sight, but fall features the most spectacular displays of color.

28. Winter Wayfaring

Winter in Zion National Park can bring a variety of weather, from clear and sunny skies to rain or snow storms, sometimes even in the same day. On balance, winter in Zion is mild and peaceful, a perfect time to explore the region in solitude.

31. The Arrival of Man

Nomadic hunters may have followed grazing animals into the region during the Ice Age, more than 11,000 years ago. The Anasazi lived in the region from 500 AD until 1200 AD when they were replaced by Paiutes.

Below: The massive sandstone monoliths of the Court of the Patriarchs in Zion Canyon on a late afternoon in autumn.
PHOTO BY GARY LADD

CAMELBACK   CANYONLANDS

Designed by Camelback Design Group, Inc., 8655 East Via de Ventura, Suite G200, Scottsdale, Arizona 85258. Phone: 602-948-4233. Distributed by Canyonlands Publications, 4860 North Ken Morey Drive, Bellemont, Arizona 86015. For ordering information please call (520) 779-3888.

Requests for additional information should be made to: Camelback/Canyonlands Venture at the address above, or call our toll free telephone number: 1-800-283-1983.

Library of Congress Catalog Number: 97-66357
International Standard Book Number: 1-879924-27-7

Proudly printed and bound in the USA.

E ven the name Zion, which by definition means an "idealized, harmonious community or utopia," fails to prepare one for the splendor of massive sandstone monoliths and graceful hardwoods of Zion Canyon. Each season unveils the spectacle of nature at its finest, accentuated by a temperate climate that seems to bring just enough, but not too much, of all the elements.

J. L. Crawford, in his excellent book *Towers of Stone*, describes Zion as a "geologic masterpiece," as apt a description as is possible. All the forces of nature have been at work here, and for a long time. Volcanic activity, faulting, wind and water created the intricate layers of rock found in Zion. Nine different formations can be seen in the rocks of the region, each a history of its time of origin, and the forces of nature present during its creation, and of the ages that have transpired since.

The Paiutes, who occupied Zion prior to the arrival of the Mormons in the 1860s, had their own name for Zion Canyon, "Ioogoon," which translates as "arrow quiver" or "come out the way you came in." While the Paiute name accurately describes the canyon, it seems to lack the sense of awe, inspiration and wonder attained by the Mormon name. This may be a result of the centuries the Paiutes spent paying tribute to the Utes from the north and suffering raids from the Navajo to the south. To the Paiutes, Zion Canyon was probably just thought of as a dead-end canyon, which could be a real problem when being pursued.

Paiutes were not the first Native Americans to inhabit Zion, they replaced the Anasazi who abandoned the region, after seven centuries of inhabitation, sometime around 1200 AD. The exact date of their departure is unknown, and they left no forwarding address. Nor did they leave remains of the multi-roomed pueblos they are famous for in other areas.

Prior to the arrival of the Anasazi, around 500 AD, earlier paleo-Indian groups are thought to have roamed through the region in pursuit of game and in search of edible plants and seeds. The very basis of the lifestyle of these nomadic hunter-gathers leaves little evidence of their occupation. They truly were here today, and gone tomorrow.

Native American occupation of Zion came to an abrupt end, when considering the centuries they had called the area home, shortly after the first Mormon missionary was sent to explore the area in hopes of finding sites for new towns for the exploding Mormon population in Utah. In 1858, a young Mormon missionary, Nephi Johnson, was first led into Zion Canyon by a group of friendly Indians, who most certainly didn't realize Nephi was the advance man for a passel of pioneers the likes of which they couldn't even imagine. By the 1860s, Mormon farms and towns were popping up everywhere, and the Indians were on their way out.

Preceding pages: The brilliant colors of Fremont cottonwoods along the banks of the Virgin River with the Pulpit in the Temple of Sinawava in the background.
PHOTO BY TERRY DONNELLY

Left: The Great White Throne, one of the most familiar landmarks in Zion National Park, rises more than 2400 feet above Zion Canyon.
PHOTO BY DICK DIETRICH

Right: Scarlet monkeyflower grows along the banks of the North Fork of the Virgin River in the Narrows in Zion Canyon National Park.
PHOTO BY LARRY ULRICH

A FEW SHORT THOUGHTS...

"The goal of life is living in agreement with Nature."

Diogenes Laertius c.400 - c.325 B.C.

"If the Earth were only a few feet in diameter, floating a few feet above a field somewhere, people would come from everywhere to marvel at it... The people would marvel at all the creatures walking around the surface of the ball and at the creatures in the water. The people would declare it sacred because it was the only one, and they would protect it so that it would not be hurt. The ball would be the greatest wonder ever known, and people would come to pray to it, to be healed, to gain knowledge, to know beauty and to wonder how it could be."

Joe Miller

"In the beginning God gave to every people a cup of clay, and from this cup they drank their life."

Paiute Proverb

"Keep a green tree in your heart and perhaps the singing bird will come."

Ancient Chinese Proverb

"Come forth into the light of things, Let Nature be your teacher."

The Tables Turned, William Wordsworth

Right: A lone ponderosa pine, *pinus ponderosa*, stands as a silent sentinel against multicolored sandstone walls at sunset in Zion.
PHOTO BY JACK DYKINGA

A FEW SHORT HIKES...

Trails among the splendor of Zion National Park are extremely rewarding as long as you remember that trails have drop-offs and it is important to remember to watch your footing. In winter, ice and snow make many trails slippery and dangerous and there may be danger from falling ice. Hiking the Narrows is not recommended in winter and early spring. Wear proper hiking attire, plan for adverse changes in weather and carry drinking water. Please stay on marked trails and leave no litter behind. Always be sure and check trail conditions with the Visitor Center before hiking.

TRAIL	STARTING POINT	ROUND TRIP	TIME	ASCENT	DEGREE OF DIFFICULTY
Pa'rus Trail	South Campground	3.5 miles 5.6 kilometers	1.5 hours	50 feet 15 meters	Easy, paved trail follows the Virgin River to Main Canyon Junction.
Weeping Rock	Zion Scenic Drive at Weeping Rock lot	0.5 miles 0.8 kilometers	0.5 hours	98 feet 30 meters	Easy, ends at Weeping rock and has hanging gardens and trailside exhibits.
Riverside Walk	Zion Scenic Drive at Temple of Sinawava	2.0 miles 3.3 kilometers	1.5 hours	57 feet 17 meters	Easy, paved trail along Virgin River has hanging gardens and trailside exhibits.
Lower Emerald Pools	Zion Scenic Drive opposite Zion Lodge	1.2 miles 1.9 kilometers	1.0 hours	69 feet 21 meters	Easy, paved trail to waterfalls and the lower pools. Accessible for disabled.
Middle Emerald Pools	Zion Scenic Drive opposite Zion Lodge	2.0 miles 3.3 kilometers	2.0 hours	150 feet 46 meters	Moderate, a loop trail to the lower and middle pools. Has long drop offs.
Canyon Overlook	Zion-Mt. Carmel Hwy east of long tunnel	1.0 miles 1.6 kilometers	1.0 hours	163 feet 50 meters	Moderate, rocky trail ends overlooking lower Zion Canyon, Pine Creek Canyon.
Watchman	East of Watchman Campground	2.0 miles 3.3 kilometers	2.0 hours	368 feet 112 meters	Moderate, ends overlooking lower Zion and Oak Creek Canyons and Springdale.
Hidden Canyon	Zion Scenic Drive at Weeping Rock lot	2.0 miles 3.2 kilometers	3.0 hours	850 feet 259 meters	Moderate, can be frightening for people afraid of heights. Long drop offs.
Sand Bench	Zion Scenic Drive opposite Zion Lodge	3.6 miles 5.8 kilometers	3.0 hours	500 feet 152 meters	Moderate, views of the Three Patriarchs and lower Zion Canyon.
Angels Landing	Zion Scenic Drive at Grotto picnic area	5.0 miles 8.6 kilometers	4.0 hours	1488 feet 453 meters	Strenuous, narrow trail, long drop-offs. Can be very dangerous when icy.
Kolob Canyons Taylor Creek	Kolob Cyns Rd 2 mi. from Visitor Center	5.0 miles 8.6 kilometers	4.0 hours	450 feet 137 meter	Moderate, follows Taylor Creek past two homesteads to Double Arch Alcove.

Compiled by Zion National Park.

ZION NATIONAL PARK GEOGRAPHY...

Geography... American Heritage Dictionary defines geography as: 1. "The study of the earth and its features and the distribution of life on the earth, including human life and the effects of human activity. 2. The geographic characteristics of an area. 3. A book on geography. 4. An ordered arrangement of constituent elements."

Zion National Park is 43 miles northeast of St. George, in southwestern Utah– 320 miles south of Salt Lake City and 158 miles northeast

LOCATION..

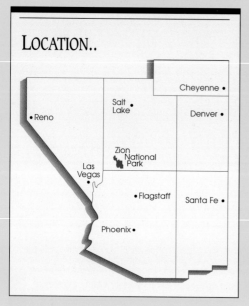

THE WEATHER FORECAST...

The chart below shows average monthly temperatures, precipitation and snowfall at Zion National Park. Weather may vary greatly in different areas of the park due to variations in elevations and exposure. Average annual precipitation is 14.40 inches. Thunderstorms are possible from April through October and common in July and August. Winters are mild with an average snowfall of around 13 inches.

Month	Average Maximum	Average Minimum	Extreme High	Extreme Low	Normal Precipitation	Maximum Snowfall
January	52°	29°	71°	-2°	1.6	26
February	57°	31°	78°	4°	1.6	18
March	63°.	36°	86°	12°	1.7	14
April	73°	43°	94°	23°	1.3	3
May	83°	52°	102°	22°	0.7	0
June	93°	60°	114°	40°	0.6	0
July	100°	68°	115°	51°	0.8	0
August	97°	66°	111°	50°	1.6	0
September	91°	60°	110°	33°	0.8	0
October	78°	49°	97°	23°	1.0	1
November	63°	37°	83°	13°	1.2	5
December	53°	30°	71°	6°	1.5	21

All temperatures above are in degrees Fahrenheit. Precipitation and snowfall are stated in inches.

Temperatures may vary 30° from day to night. Spring weather varies; summer is warm with afternoon thunderstorms; fall is clear and mild with colors beginning to change in September.

Source: Data summaries compiled by Zion National Park.

of Las Vegas, Nevada. This remote location was responsible for the area's late settlement by Europeans. It was not until 1858 that Mormon leader Brigham Young sent a young missionary to the area in search of natural resources and potential sites for further Mormon towns. The missionary, a young man named Nephi Johnson, was lead by a group of Indians into the canyon, which he explored in search of suitable farm land. It is unknown how far into Zion Canyon he traveled. By some accounts he traveled as far as the Great White Throne, by others, to the entrance to the Narrows.

During the early 1860s hundreds of Mormon families began to settle the areas surrounding Zion. By 1861, crops were being raised and herds were being grazed in Zion Canyon.

A HOP, SKIP, AND A JUMP...

Distances from the Zion Visitor Center to popular western United States destinations by automobile:

DESTINATION	MILES	KILOMETERS
Bryce Canyon, NP	86	138
Cedar Breaks, NM	76	122
Death Valley, NP	297	475
Glen Canyon, NRA	115	185
Grand Canyon, NP	120	193
Lake Mead, NRA	189	304
Las Vegas, NV	158	254
Phoenix, AZ	422	679
Pipe Springs, NM	63	101
Salt Lake City, UT	320	515
San Francisco, CA	726	1168
Yosemite NP, CA	543	874

Left: Zion Canyon and the Virgin River from Observation Point in April.
PHOTO: TOM TILL

Zion National Park has a temperate climate. Although spring can be unpredictable, with every day capable of anything from rain-to-snow-to-sunshine, summer's days are warm, with highs above 90°, but nights are mild with temperatures in the 60's and 70's. Fall brings

year, in 1919, Stephen Tyng Mather, the first director of the National Park Service, used his considerable influence and congressional support to have Zion declared a national park.

During the 1920s, tourism found southern Utah and lodges were built by the Utah Parks Company, a division of the Union Pacific Railroad, in Zion Canyon, Bryce Canyon and Cedar Breaks. In 1930, the Zion– Mt. Carmel Tunnel,

which bores 1.1 miles though solid rock, was completed shortening the distance between Zion and points east, including saving 70 miles in travel distance between Zion National Park and Bryce Canyon National Park.

Today, nearly 150,000 acres of Zion National Park receive around 2.6 million visitors each year, a testimony to the dedication of the men and women of our National Park Service.

ZION CANYON...

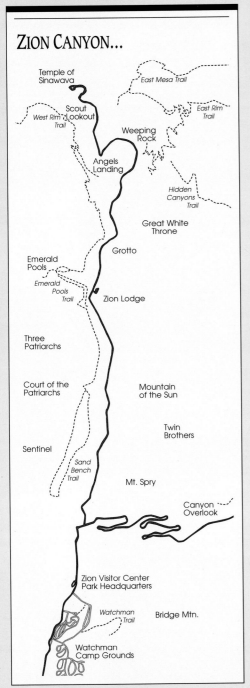

a spectacular change of colors with mild and clear weather. Winter is normally mild but may bring icy roads.

Zion National Park was first established as the Mukuntuweap National Monument by a proclamation of President William Howard Taft in 1909. In 1918, the Mukuntuweap name, hard to pronounce and unpopular with almost everyone, was changed to Zion. The following

DISTANCES TO LOCAL ATTRACTIONS...

Mileages from the Zion Canyon Visitor Center to destinations within and around Zion National Park by automobile are as follows:
Source: National Park Service, Zion National Park

DESTINATION	MILES	DESTINATION	MILES	DESTINATION	MILES
1. Cedar City	60	6. Lava Point	40	11. St. George	42
2. East Entrance	13	7. La Verkin	20	12. Temple of Sinawava	7
3. Emerald Pools	3	8. Mt. Carmel Junction	25	13. Watchman Campground	1
4. Grotto	4	9. South Entrance	1	14. Weeping Rock	6
5. Kolob Canyons	45	10. Springdale	2	15. Zion Lodge	3

TRAILHEADS

16. Angels Landing		22. Hidden Canyon	
17. Canyon Overlook		23. Kolob Canyons	
18. Chinle		24. Pa'rus Trail	
19. East Mesa		25. Sand Bench	
20. East Rim		26. Riverside Walk	
21. Emerald Pools		27. Watchman	
		28. West Rim	

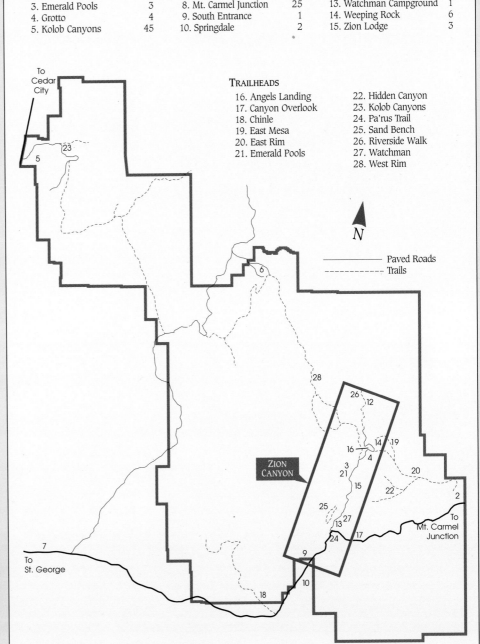

Paved Roads
Trails

The geology of Zion is truly a unique study. Here, all of nature's forces have been in effect creating a landscape that is unlike any other. The geology of Zion lay deep within the nine layers of sedimentary rock formations deposited here over the past 240 million years.

Zion is the middle step in the Grand Staircase, a series of geologic layers that were uplifted and rise in a stair-like fashion from the Grand Canyon in the south, to Bryce Canyon in the north. The Pink Cliffs, where the whimsical formations of Bryce Canyon were formed in the deposits of the Claron Formation, form the northernmost step of the Grand Staircase and expose the youngest geologic deposits. These deposits were deposited during the Paleocene epoch, between 54 and 65 million years ago.

Between Bryce Canyon and Zion, the Grey Cliffs, the second step on the Grand Staircase, expose deposits that are between 120 and 135 million years old. Zion exposes the formations of the White Cliffs, sedimentary deposits that were formed around 165 million years ago.

The Vermilion Cliffs, with formations 165 to 200 million years old, lie between Zion and Grand Canyon, as do the Chocolate Cliffs with deposits 200 to 225 million years old.

At the Grand Canyon, the southernmost step in the staircase, the oldest deposits are exposed. Kaibab Plateau deposits, part of the Grand Canyon's North Rim, are around 250 million years old and are the lowest step on the Grand Staircase. Kaibab deposits are the youngest in the Grand Canyon and reach thicknesses of 300–500 feet. The oldest formations exposed in the Grand Canyon's lowest reaches, Vishnu Schist and Zoraster Granite, accumulated more than two billion years ago.

The nine formations at Zion were laid one on top of another and are, in order from the youngest (top or highest), the Dakota, Carmel, Temple Cap, Navajo, Kayenta, Moenave, Chinle, Moenkopi and Kaibab. The oldest deposits, the Kaibab, were, of course, laid first and are on the bottom layer of this nine layer cake.

Kaibab formations are the oldest deposits in Zion, formed during the Middle Permian period of the Paleozoic era (see chart page 13). The Kaibab Formation, not a prominent feature in Zion, can be found in Timpoweap Canyon and in the Hurricane Cliffs.

The Moenkopi Formation was laid during the Early Triassic period of the Mesozoic era and is composed of thousands of thin sandstone and shale layers. The Moenkopi Formation contains deposits of oil bearing shale, limestone and gypsum that show bright bands of red, pink, white and gray that were laid at the bottom of an ancient sea.

The Chinle Formation was deposited in the Late Triassic period of the Mesozoic era and is between 400–500 feet thick in Zion National Park. It shows purple, white and gray shales

Left: Ponderosa pine at Checkerboard Mesa in Zion National Park. Checkerboard Mesa is the result of differential erosion along horizontal bedding planes. Frost wedging, a process by which water enters cracks in rocks, freezes, causing it to expand and pry rock apart, has caused the uncommon vertical lines.
PHOTO BY LARRY ULRICH

Right: Hoodoos on slickrock sandstone beneath the White Cliffs. Hoodoos are erosional remains of rocks in whimsical shapes, normally caused as less resistant rock below is protected by a caprock of harder material.
PHOTO BY TERRY DONNELLY

GEOLOGY CONTINUED...

with light colored layers of sandstone and limestone. The Chinle Formation also contains the Petrified Forest, bands of which are seen at the park's south entrance and by Springdale.

The Moenave Formation was deposited in the Late Triassic or Early Jurassic periods of the Mesozoic era and is comprised of siltstone, sandstone and mudstone and is thought to have been deposited at the bottom of a lake. Streams, rivers and ponds deposited additional material after the lake dried up. It is thought that an equatorial climate existed in Zion during this period.

The Kayenta Formation was deposited during the Early Jurassic period of the Mesozoic era as siltstones and sandstones. The tightly cemented quartz grains of this formation are impervious and force water seeping from the upper deposits to travel horizontally until they escape as either springs or seeps. The Kayenta Formation forms the "spring line" on Zion's canyon walls.

The most prominent formation in Zion is the Navajo Formation, from which Zion Canyon is carved and the park's formations are made. This fine-grained sandstone reaches maximum thickness, almost 2400 feet, at the Temple of Sinawava. Throughout Zion National Park it averages between 1500 and 2000 feet thick.

Navajo Formation deposits are cemented by

THE GRAND STAIRCASE...

The Grand Staircase is a series of geologic formations that rise in a stair-like fashion from the Grand Canyon to Bryce Canyon. The Pink Cliffs of Bryce Canyon form the northern step of the Grand Staircase, with the youngest geologic deposits. Situated between Bryce and Zion, the Grey Cliffs expose rocks between 120 and 135 million years old. Zion exposes the White Cliffs, deposited about 165 million years ago.

The Vermilion Cliffs, with deposits 165 to 200 million years old, lie between Zion and the Grand Canyon, as do the Chocolate Cliffs with deposits 200 to 225 million years old. The Grand Canyon, the southernmost step in the staircase, exposes rock from 250 million to 1.7 billion years old.

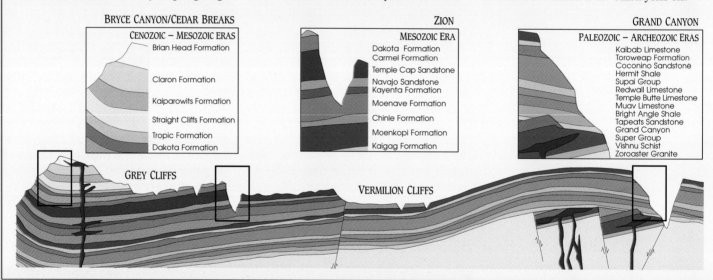

BRYCE CANYON/CEDAR BREAKS

CENOZOIC – MESOZOIC ERAS

- Brian Head Formation
- Claron Formation
- Kaiparowits Formation
- Straight Cliffs Formation
- Tropic Formation
- Dakota Formation

ZION

MESOZOIC ERA

- Dakota Formation
- Carmel Formation
- Temple Cap Sandstone
- Navajo Sandstone
- Kayenta Formation
- Moenave Formation
- Chinle Formation
- Moenkopi Formation
- Kaigag Formation

GRAND CANYON

PALEOZOIC – ARCHEOZOIC ERAS

- Kaibab Limestone
- Toroweap Formation
- Coconino Sandstone
- Hermit Shale
- Supai Group
- Redwall Limestone
- Temple Butte Limestone
- Muav Limestone
- Bright Angle Shale
- Tapeats Sandstone
- Grand Canyon Super Group
- Vishnu Schist
- Zoroaster Granite

GREY CLIFFS

VERMILION CLIFFS

iron oxides, clays and lime, which are very weak bonding agents. The weakness of the cement in Navajo Formation deposits allows its easy erosion into the features present in the park. Wind, in addition to water, has shaped the Navajo Formation deposits at Zion. Fantastic cross-bedded deposits, parallel deposits at odd angles, stair steps, sweeping arcs and other strange layers of deposits seen in the park are often Navajo Sandstone.

The Temple Cap Formation was deposited in the Mid Jurassic period of the Mesozoic era as a thin deposit of red mud. It is seen in Zion as the caprock at both East Temple and West Temple.

The Carmel Formation was deposited in the Mid Jurassic period of the Mesozoic era and is comprised of tan and grey limestones, red clay and tan and light pink sandstones. Carmel deposits have marine origins with snails and bivalves found in limestone deposits. Small fragments of igneous rock have been found in the Carmel Formation that do not appear to have their edges rounded off, evidence that may lead to this period as the beginning of volcanic activity in the region.

The Dakota Formation was deposited in the Cretaceous period of the Mesozoic era. It is not found in the park except in a small area of the northwest corner although it is seen to the north and east of the park. It was during this period that great changes began to take place in the entire region of the Colorado Plateau.

Around 16 million years ago, a collision of the earth's plates along the west coast of North America uplifted the entire Colorado Plateau. The plateau rose slowly from the south, giving the region a downward south-north slope. As the slope increased, gentle streams and lazy rivers that originally laid sedimentary deposits in the region were transformed into raging

ABOUT TIME...

Geology is the scientific study of the origin, history, and structure of the earth. All studies are based on the division and the sub-division of historical geology into eras, periods and epochs...

PRECAMBRIAN	BEGINNING	ENDING
Archeozoic	older than 4 billion years	
Proterozoic	4 billion	600
PALEOZOIC		
Cambrian	600	500
Ordovician	500	425
Silurian	425	400
Devonian	400	345
Mississippian	345	320
Pennsylvanian	320	280
Permian	280	225
MESOZOIC		
Triassic	225	190
Jurassic	190	135
Cretaceous	135	65
CENOZOIC		
TERTIARY		
Paleocene	65	54
Eocene	54	38
Oligocene	38	26
Miocene	26	12
Pliocene	12	1.7
QUATERNARY		
Pleistocene	1.7	10,000 years
Holocene	10,000 years to present	

torrents of water and began eroding sedimentary layers. Rivers, streams and running water, fed by rain and melting snow, are still responsible for downcutting that continues to erode the Markagunt Plateau.

Chemical weathering is caused as mineral laden solutions penetrate cracks and crevices and accelerate erosion by breaking rocks into smaller pieces, which are more easily removed by running water. Solutions of seeping water penetrate weaker layers of rock and dissolve the calcium-carbonate cement that binds the individual grains, turning rock into sand.

Frost wedging forces rock apart as rainwater or snow melt seeps inside, freezes, expands its volume which subsequently exerts tremendous pressure and pries the rock apart. Erosion is also caused by organic weathering, occurring as expanding roots of plants and trees pry rock apart. Or, as animals burrow into rock to create a living space thus contributing to the breakdown as they chip away at the structural strength of canyon walls.

When hiking in Zion National Park remain on trails to reduce your impact on the canyon's natural features. And for your own safety, stay away from cliffs and steep slopes which can be extremely dangerous due to the loose sands and gravels inherent in the park's soft sandstone formations.

The canyons of Zion are the direct result of ongoing erosion of the Markagunt Plateau by the Virgin River and its tributaries, which work constantly to carve themselves ever deeper into the soft sandstones of the plateau.

Below: A full moon shines down on West Temple and the Towers of the Virgin.
PHOTO BY JEFF FOOTT

Below: Wet sandstone reflects the sky in Zion. Navajo Formation deposits in the park average between 1500 and 2000 feet in thickness.
PHOTO BY LARRY ULRICH

Above: A gnarled pine, tilted hoodoo and walls of cross-bedded, multi-colored Navajo sandstone in Zion National Park.
PHOTO BY TERRY DONNELLY

Right: Striated lines on Navajo sandstone, the prominent geologic formation in Zion National Park and a Fremont cottonwood in fall.
PHOTO BY TERRY DONNELLY

The Virgin River, at times appearing only a gentle stream and at others a roiling torrent, has been the primary force in carving Zion Canyon through the horizontal layers of rock of the Markagunt Plateau. As the Virgin River flows through the canyon it is responsible for eroding its bed to ever deeper levels. The rock and sand it carries along add to its downcutting power as rock downstream is broken down from boulders to rocks, rocks to cobbles, cobbles to pebbles, pebbles to grains of sand and finally, from grains of sand to silt.

This process of downcutting has continued for every minute of every day for millions of years. At times, after long dry spells, the Virgin River may flow at the relatively gentle rate of 20 feet per second, still downcutting and moving debris downstream, but without the force necessary to move boulders and rocks. Other times, when the river is in flood, it may move at ten times its normal flow (normal flow is around 100 cubic feet per second) with force enough to dislodge huge boulders and send them downstream, or undercut layers of its banks. It has been estimated that at normal flow the river removes enough silt every day to fill thirty dump trucks– a dump truck carries 4 cubic yards of material.

Tributaries to the Virgin River flow through narrow canyons that are nearly all rock. With little to impede the water's progress as it rushes to the Virgin River, and the river's steep 76 foot per mile average gradient through Zion Canyon, it sends a torrent of water at great speed through the canyon in times of spring runoff or following rain storms. In times of flood it is estimated that a flood of ten times the normal flow removes up to 2000 times as much material. More than one million tons of rock debris (rock, sand and silt) are removed by the Virgin River each year, the bulk of which is the result of flooding.

In addition to downcutting Zion Canyon, the Virgin River also assists in its widening. Aided by fine-grained and soft rock formations that easily disintegrate, rainwater enters porous sandstone weakening the elements binding it together and then seeping from the walls as evidenced at the Grotto, Weeping Rock and areas where springs or seeps have undermined upper layers of deposits leaving overhanging cliffs. Fault lines and joints in cliff formations aid in the canyon's erosion as frost wedging, chemical and mechanical weathering, and running water pry rock apart along bedding planes until blocks and slabs are sent crashing to the canyon floor. Rain and wind beat against canyon walls and send particles of rock and sand to the canyon floor, where it eventually washes into the Virgin River and is carried away.

Although the Virgin River carves deeper into Zion Canyon by only a few millimeters each year, it has had millions of years to sculpt the canyon in a process that continues today.

Left: The Virgin River flows through Zion Canyon on a stormy October day. The muddy appearance of the river gives testament to the large amounts of silt the river carries.
PHOTO BY GARY LADD

Right: The Virgin River plunges through Zion Canyon in mid-November. The normal flow of the river is 100 cubic feet per second although in times of flood it may increase by as much as ten times, creating enough force to move large rocks and boulders downstream.
PHOTO BY LARRY ULRICH

WATER WORKS...

Right: Waterfall at Pine Creek on an April afternoon in Pine Creek Canyon. As creeks and rivers cut through canyons they remove loose materials by the force of their water and use the materials they dislodge to break other rock into pieces small enough to move along downstream. Stream bedload is the loose cobbles, gravel and sand found lying on the bottom when water levels are low. As water levels increase, the bedload grinds the bedrock of the stream to lower levels.
PHOTO BY JEFF GNASS

Above: As the Left Fork of North Creek emerges from The Subway it flows down terraced layers of rock at Archangel Cascade.
PHOTO BY LARRY ULRICH

Above: Fall colors adorn hardwoods beside the Virgin River along the Gateway to the Narrows Trail. Blocks and slabs of rock in the river have crashed down from canyon walls above, a result of erosion along cracks caused by frost wedging, weathering and running water.
PHOTO BY TERRY DONNELLY

Above: As water soaks into porous sandstone it permeates the rock until it reaches lower deposits that are too hard to penetrate. It then moves in a horizontal fashion until it emerges from canyon walls as a spring or seep, as illustrated in this photograph of Weeping Rock.
PHOTO BY DICK DIETRICH

Left: Blue skies are reflected in the Virgin River below the Watchman in early October. The Virgin River flows around 160 miles before it enters Lake Mead and the Colorado River.
PHOTO BY RANDY PRENTICE

Right: Waterfall above Lower Emerald Pool. Two waterfalls at Emerald Pools have created a small canyon, across the highway from Zion Lodge, by eroding the Navajo Formation.
PHOTO BY LARRY ULRICH

WILDLIFE...

Zion National Park's unique landscape, with its shaded canyon walls, hanging gardens and riparian (streamside) biotic communities supports a variety of wildlife from the Sonoran, Transition and Canadian lifezones. Diversity of animal life found within the park is even more unique when considering the overlap of species from each zone found in settings that are not normally their preferred habitats. In Zion, exposure to sunlight and moisture is more important than changes in elevation in determining habitats.

More than 70 species of mammals can be found in Zion including three shrew species; vagrant, northern water and desert (or gray) shrews, fifteen species of bats; from the little brown myotis, *Myotis lucifugus,* found in coniferous forests to the big freetail bat, *Tadarida molossa,* and pallid bat, *Antrozous pallidus,* found in the canyons. Three rabbit species; blacktail jackrabbit, *Lepus californicus,* mountain cottontail, *Sylvilagus nuttallii,* and the desert cottontail, *Sylvilagus audubonii,* are found along with the America pika, *Ochotona princeps,* short-eared, short-limbed tailless relatives of the rabbit with a close appearance to guinea pigs.

The rodent family is well represented, with 34 species ranging from the least chipmunk, *Tamias minimus,* Uinta chipmunk, *Tamias umbrinus,* rock squirrel, *Spermophilus variegatus,* white-tailed antelope squirrel, *Ammospermophilus leucurus,* and northern flying

Above: A coyote, *Canis latrans*, walking in snow. Coyotes are fairly common year-round and can be found parkwide. PHOTO BY LEN RUE, JR.

Above: Gambel's quail, *Lophortyx gambelii,* are common residents throughout the year and can be found in desert areas, canyon bottomlands, fields, meadows and riparian woodlands of the Virgin River and its many tributaries.
PHOTO BY LEN RUE, JR.

REINTRODUCTION OF THE DESERT BIGHORN...

The desert bighorn is well suited to the more remote areas of Zion National Park and surrounding regions, able to exist for several days without water and feeding on a wide variety of grasses and plants.

Desert bighorn are shy animals usually seen only by adventurous hikers exploring remote areas. The spectacular curved horns of mature males may reach as much as 36 inches in length with a circumference of up to 14 inches at the base. The majestic horns of the bighorn– a measure of status in the herd, where only males with horns of equal length will fight, are unfortunately quite popular with hunters who prize the rams for the trophies their horns provide and have helped drive the desert bighorn to near extinction.

In Zion National Park and surrounding regions the decline of the desert bighorn, thought to have been the indigenous bighorn of the area, was the result of human development in the region. As domestic grazing animals– sheep, cattle and horses– were introduced and began to compete with the bighorn for forage and access to water they also introduced diseases previously unknown in desert bighorn. The Rocky Mountain bighorn, *Ovis canadensis canadensis,* was also once found in southern Utah but has long been completely extirpated throughout the region.

Bighorn range was further decreased during the 1920s by construction of Zion-Mt. Carmel Highway, which divided their range in half. During the 1930s, Zion National Park officials reduced estimates of desert bighorn population to a mere 25 animals. The herd decreased until its last member was spotted in 1953, only to disappear a short time later.

Reintroduction of the desert bighorn began in 1964, fueled by a National Park Service policy that allowed missing native life forms to be

Above: Desert bighorn, *Ovis canadensis nelsoni,* are thought to have been the indigenous bighorn of the Zion area prior to being completely eliminated by human activities by 1953. PHOTO BY LEN RUE, JR.

reestablished. In July of 1973, after nearly a decade of effort, twelve desert bighorn that had been captured in Nevada were released into a large enclosed area near the Visitor Center. The plan was to give the bighorn time to establish social bonds, increase their numbers and get used to their new environment prior to their release into the wild.

In 1976, thirteen members of the herd, then numbering 22 animals, were released in remote Parunuweap Canyon. A year later researchers determined that four bighorn ewes had returned to the familiarity of the enclosed area and five had fallen prey to mountain lions, which they were unfamiliar with, or to disease. In June of 1978, after the herd had increased to twenty members, the enclosed area was opened and the bighorn were allowed to roam freely, a more successful release than the previous attempt.

Today, more than 65 bighorn comprise the Zion population, thanks to the efforts of the National Park Service reintroduction program.

squirrel, *Glaucomys sabrinus,* to the larger members of the rodent family including the yellow-bellied marmot, *Marmota flaviventris,* North American beaver, *Castor canadensis,* common muskrat, *Ondatra zibethica,* and the porcupine, *Erethizon dorsatum.*

The park's rodent species feed on a variety of plants, insects and seeds and are prey for carnivores including coyote, *Canis latrans,* kit fox, *Vulpes velox,* common grey fox, *Urocyon cinereoargenteus,* red fox, *vulpes vulpes,* black bear, *Ursus americanus,* ringtail, *Bassariscus astutus,* long-tailed weasel, *Mustela frenata,* badger, *Taxidea taxus,* western spotted skunk, *Spilogale gracilis,* striped skunk *Mephitis mephitis,* mountain lion, *Felis concolor,* and bobcat, *Lynx rufus.* Grizzly bear, *Ursus arctos,* and grey wolf, *Canis lupus,* were once found in the area but were extirpated (completely removed) by earlier inhabitants.

The larger carnivores also prey on the area's hooved mammals which include mule deer,

rattlesnake, *Crotalus viridis lutosus,* which can be found in elevations below 8000 ft. throughout the park.

Zion provides habitat for more than 270 bird species including red-tailed hawk, Cooper's hawk, Swainson's hawk, rough-legged hawk, osprey, bald eagle, golden eagle, merlin, prairie falcon, peregrine falcon, barn owl, great horned owl, Mexican spotted owl, western screech owl, turkey, belted kingfisher, great blue heron, snowy egret, downy woodpecker, northern flicker, willow flycatcher, Hammond's flycatcher, gray flycatcher, Cassin's kingbird, horned lark, Steller's Jay, pinyon jay, common raven, rock wren, canyon wren, Canada goose, wood duck, green-winged teal, cinnamon teal, ruddy duck, American wigeon, common merganser, northern pintail, Virginia rail, least sandpiper, mourning dove, western grebe, yellow-billed cuckoo, greater roadrunner, barn swallow, American robin, hermit thrush, blue grosbeak, western tanager, cedar waxwing, black-chinned hummingbird and more than two hundred other colorful avian species.

Below: Mountain lion, *felis concolor,* or cougar, are the largest North American cats. A mature cougar can make a running leap of up to 39 feet.
PHOTO BY LEN RUE, JR.

Above: North American beaver, *Castor canadensis,* feeding along a river bank. By the late 1800s, the beaver had disappeared from regions around Zion National Park. Sometime in the late 1930s or early 1940s they returned, migrating up the Colorado River to the Virgin River. The beavers in Zion National Park normally dig burrows in river banks instead of attempting to dam the fast moving waters of the Virgin River and its tributaries. Beavers live in close family groups including a male, female and their young.
PHOTO BY LEN RUE, JR.

Odocoileus hemionus, which are a common sight throughout the park, elk, *Cervus elaphus,* occasionally seen in higher elevations, and desert bighorn, *Ovis canadensis nelsoni,* which were extirpated but have been reintroduced (see sidebar page 20).

Above: A male and female cinnamon teal, *Anas cyanoptera.* These small surface feeding ducks are known to breed in calm water areas of Zion National Park and surrounding regions, although they are not a common sight.
PHOTO BY LEN RUE, JR.

Zion National Park is also home to more than twenty five species of reptiles including many colorful species of lizards, skinks and snakes including the poisonous Great Basin

Zion National Park features a surprising variety of plant communities, a result of varying elevations, access to water and exposure to the sun. In the study of ecology, a science dealing with all living things, seven life zones were established between the equator and the North Pole in a study of flora and fauna formulated during the late nineteenth century by Clinton Hart Merriam for the U.S. Department of Agriculture. Merriam's study was based on the premise that a change of 1000 feet in elevation will have the same effect on plant life as changes of 300–500 miles in latitude. Merriam also determined temperature drops 3.5 to 5 degrees for each 1000 foot rise in elevation. The high temperatures and dry weather of Zion cause an overlap of species that is uncommon, plants normally found in a specific life zone may be found in areas not usually associated with the species.

Zion National Park contains several distinct life zones, or plant communities. In elevations below 5000 feet plants of the Sonoran Zone can be found. The Sonoran Zone is home to the pinyon-juniper forests, sometimes called pygmy or dwarf forests for the stunted appearance of their trees. Here, single-leaf pinyon, *Pinus monophylla,* and Utah juniper, *Juniperus osteosperma,* dominate, adding their evergreen presence to manzanita, *Arctostaphylos manzanita,* singleleaf ash, *Fraxinus anomala,* Utah serviceberry, *Amelanchier alnifolia,* Gambel oak, *Quercus gambelii,* bigtooth maple, *Acer grandidentatum,* cliffrose, *Cowania mexicana,* Mormon tea, *Ephedra viridis,* and buffaloberry, *Shepherdia canadenis.* Also found in Sonoran zones, both the Upper and Lower Sonoran Life Zones, are several cacti species including various hedgehogs, prickly pears and chollas.

There are no hard-fast boundaries between different life zones and species occasionally mingle as slope exposure (the direction a slope faces) changes the life zone's normal limits. Each of these habitats generally support a diversity of flora and fauna that have adapted to the conditions and challenges of life found within the individual life zones.

In Zion Canyon, and neighboring canyons, various riparian (literally pertaining to the bank of a natural course of water) woodland communities can be found supporting Fremont cottonwood, *Populus Fremontii,* velvet ash, *Fraxinus velutina,* black birch, *Betula occidentalis,* Boxelder, *Acer negundo,* and bigtooth maple, *Acer grandidentatum,* along the banks of the Virgin River and its tributaries. These deciduous trees create a magical environment from spring through autumn with a continual show of color against steep canyon walls.

Occupation of the canyon by Europeans has had a major impact on many of the life zones and especially on riparian plant communities. Native species have been replaced by exotic species. Tamarisk, *Tamarix chinensis,* or salt

Left: Boxelder, *Acer negundo,* also known as ashleaf maple, against a Navajo sandstone wall in Kolobs Canyon that has been streaked with desert varnish. Desert varnish, appearing wet but dry to the touch, is the result of iron oxide stains on rock surfaces. In places desert varnish gains a purple hue, the result of manganese in addition to iron.
PHOTO BY JACK DYKINGA

Right: Fremont cottonwoods, *Populus Fremontii,* frame the Great White Throne in Zion Canyon on a crystal-clear November afternoon. These magnificent trees grow to heights of 80 feet.
PHOTO BY JEFF GNASS

cedar, has formed dense thickets and choked out many less hardy species in its aggressive quest for access to water.

Above: Leopard Lily, *Lilium paralinum,* in Clear Creek Canyon. Scant rainfall and high temperatures in Zion cause two growing cycles, spring and late summer, for wildflower species. PHOTO BY LARRY ULRICH

Elevations in the Transition Zone, from 5500 to 7500 feet, feature forests of ponderosa pine, *Pinus ponderosa,* quaking aspen, *Populus tremuloides,* Douglas fir, *Pseudotsuga menziesii,* white fir, *Abies concolor,* Gambel oak, *Quercus gambelii,* and the rarer Rocky Mountain juniper, *Juniperus scopulorum.* With increased moisture from rainfall and snowmelt, along with its more moderate temperatures, the Transition Zone supports a greater variety of flora and fauna than the park's other life zones.

Here, ponderosa pines form stately stands with some specimens reaching heights of 130 feet and existing as long as 500 years. The ponderosa pine have extensive root systems to capture moisture from the soil, discouraging close growth from other plants.

Because Zion Canyon is considered a desert canyon it is not unusual to find several species of cacti and four species of yucca on exposed slopes, even in the highest elevations of the Transition Zone. Although yucca resemble cactus, they belong to the lily family. Spring brings the yucca to bloom as it shoots its stalk skyward. Native Americans had many uses for the yucca; as a food source, a fiber source to weave mats, baskets and sandals, and as a building material.

The Native American inhabitants were able to harvest the bounty of Zion's forests and canyons without causing their destruction, unlike the European pioneers who decimated large tracts of land when they cut trees for lumber and severely over-grazed meadows for use as pastures for sheep and cattle.

Zion offers several very special plant communities including hanging gardens, places where calcareous tufa– a porous limestone formed as calcium carbonate is deposited as water leaches from canyon walls– exists and

Slickrock paintbrush, *Castilleja scabrida,* grows in a crevice of Navajo sandstone in Zion Canyon at Zion National Park. Four species of red paintbrush can be found in various habitats of Zion. PHOTO BY TOM DANIELSEN

SACRED DATURA...

This member of the nightshade family is probably one of the most interesting plants found in Zion National Park. It features the largest blooms of any plant in southern Utah, between 5 and 8 inches long and just as wide with single plants that may have as many as 100 blooms. Because the blooms only open at night, a common name for the sacred datura is "moon lily." The plant is so common in Zion they are also called "Zion lily."

The sacred datura is very poisonous. All parts of the plant are poisonous, containing different alkaloids (complex chemical compounds) that can be poisonous when they are combined or taken alone. Scopolamine and atropine are the primary alkaloids. Native Americans used sacred datura and the hallucinogenic effects its alkaloids produced in religious ceremonies.

Sacred datura has been used to treat asthma, prevent miscarriages, as a relaxant and as an anesthetic. Because of the high levels of toxicity in the plants– some are much more toxic than others as alkaloids in the plant are absorbed by its roots from soil and distributed throughout the rest of the plant in varying amounts depending on where the plant grows– it is extremely dangerous to ingest any part of the plant. They are known to cause loss of sight, convulsions, incoherent speech, delirium and death. The plant is so toxic that no species of animals graze on it.

Sacred datura grow in dry, sandy soils and areas that have been disturbed (burned areas, along side roads, construction areas etc).

Sacred Datura, *Datura Wrightii Regel,* flowers with large showy white blooms, largest of any flowering plant in southern Utah. In bloom from early spring through fall, Sacred Datura only opens its blossoms at night, which is probably just as well since they are extremely poisonous. PHOTO BY TOM TILL

They can be found in park elevations between 3500 and 7000 feet and their white blooms can be seen from early spring through fall.

water seeps from the walls to support maidenhair fern, three species of columbine, several species of monkeyflower, and showy shooting stars along with grasses, mosses and lichens.

Moist and wet areas of Zion National Park feature a variety of plants including five-finger and maidenhair ferns, horsetail, several species of sedges and rushes, orchids– most common of which is the giant helleborine– and miner's lettuce, which is found in wet and shady areas. Also found are three species of columbine, seven species of buttercup, water cress, shooting star, several species of monkeyflower, cardinal flower and alumroot.

Dry areas include spiderwort, several species of lily– including Sego lily which blooms late in spring, two species of death camas and false Solomon seal– buckwheat and slickrock sulfurflower which flower in fall. Wild rhubarb is common in the lower canyon and Russian thistle, the familiar tumbleweed, can be found in dry floodplains.

Showy red-violet four o'clocks can be seen in late afternoon and evening along with several species of evening primrose, flowering in white, yellow or pink, and the sacred datura, *Datura wrightii regel,* also known as the moon lily or Zion lily, which blossoms late at night in elevations between 3500 and 7000 feet.

Two species of sand verbena can be found in sandy areas, three species of larkspur await in higher elevations and seven species of

bloom any time of year except during winter, as does golden aster. Eleven cryptantha species can be found in dry areas along with several sunflowers and flannel mullein.

Milkvetch species can be found throughout the park as can deerclover in the sandy or rocky areas. Four aster species bloom in the fall showing white through purple flowers as do two species of purple tansy-aster.

Yarrow can be seen in bloom in July on the high plateaus and the park's several species of senecio can be found in bloom in spring or fall.

Above: Purple sage, *Salvia dorrii,* also called desert sage, on Moquitch Hill in Zion Canyon. A member of the mint family, purple sage is not a sagebrush. The plant's purplish bracts and blue flowers give off a very pleasant fragrance in May and June. This species differs from the one described by Zane Grey in his famous "Riders of the Purple Sage" by a few minor technical details.   PHOTO BY LARRY ULRICH

Above: A waterfall flows from a spring into a cool, dark grotto in a narrow side canyon. The rocks of the grotto are covered with maidenhair fern, monkeyflower and mosses.
PHOTO BY TOM TILL

buttercup can be found (some are also found in wet areas). Wallflower is a common mustard with showy yellow flowers in spring and can be seen in the canyons and on plateaus.

Around ten species of lupine, some of which are very showy, three species of mallow with orange flowers, several species of phlox and spectacular species of penstemon can be seen throughout the park. Meadows and cooler canyons find wild flax blooming in May and June. Puccoon shows bright yellow flowers in spring, which also show skyrocket's long scarlet flowers in bloom. Ground-hugging filaree can be found with its red/violet flowers in

Right: The sun sets on The Watchman and a field of Oxeye daisy, one of twelve daisy species found in Zion National Park.
PHOTO BY TOM TILL

The Festival of Fall...

Magnificent hardwoods in Zion Canyon illustrate the turning of the seasons– from the first subtle colors of spring; to the full-leaved and bright greens of summer; to splashy show of fall colors; to stark absence of foliage during the dead of winter. Of all seasons, even considering the promise of things to come during spring, fall always features the most spectacular and dramatic displays of color in the life cycle of a plant.

Fall represents the culmination of the life cycle of a leaf. Before a leaf falls from the tree, all its valuable remaining minerals and nutrients are transported from the leaf into the tree to avoid their loss. As soon as this process begins, the leaf stops producing chlorophyll, the substance that is responsible for its green color, to conserve energy and existing nutrients left in the leaf.

As the chlorophyll gradually fades away, the other pigments that were present in the leaf begin to show through. The yellow colors we see are the product of xanthophyll, while the red and orange colors are created by the presence of carotene, minerals that gain vibrancy as the chlorophyll fades.

Fall color is further enhanced by chemical reactions in the leaf producing anthocyanins, resulting in blue, scarlet or purple pigments, manufactured from the sugars that remain in the leaf after the nutrient supply has been denied. As the colors of anthocyanins are added to the xanthophyll and carotenes, they blend to create the full spectrum of fall colors.

The process of renewal in the plant's life cycle begins anew as its discarded leaves fall to the ground surrounding its own roots. The cast off and decomposing leaves contain large amounts of mineral salts– including sulfur, iron, calcium, phosphorous, potassium, magnesium and other elements essential to the rebirth of the plant during

Above: September colors of bigtooth maple in the Narrows of the Virgin River in Zion National Park. PHOTO BY GARY LADD

the following spring. As the leaves decay on the ground above the plant's roots, their minerals seep into the soil and are absorbed by the root system. Nature's own fertilizer.

Leaves begin changing colors in the early fall as photoperiodism– a phenomenon timing the major events in the lives of plants such as their flowering, the opening leaf buds and the appearance of fruit– sends a signal to the plant to start the chemical changes that in turn begin to alter the leaf's color.

Photosynthesis, the chemical process that gives plants the ability to produce glucose for use as their own food using a combination of water, light, carbon dioxide and heat is stopped until spring brings forth a new crop of leaves, to once again begin manufacturing chlorophyll and complete the cycle.

Above: Fall colors show details of bigtooth maple, *Acer grandidentatum,* and Gambel oak, *Quercus gambelii,* in Zion Canyon. PHOTO BY TERRY DONNELLY

Left: Autumn splendor along the Virgin River in Zion Canyon during November.
PHOTO BY JEFF GNASS

Right: Showy fall colors of Fremont cottonwood, *Populus fremontii,* and bigtooth maple, *Acer grandidentatum,* in brilliant contrast to canyon walls in the wash under the Weeping Rock.
PHOTO BY TERRY DONNELLY

WINTER WAYFARING...

Winter in Zion National Park can bring a variety of weather, from clear and sunny skies to rain storms or snow storms, sometimes even in the same day. On balance, winters in the park are mild, with daily high temperatures averaging in the mid 50's and with daily lows barely below freezing at an average of 30° F.

This is not to say winter storms are taken lightly. In fact, as much as 1.5–2.0 feet of snow may fall during the winter months, although seasonal average snowfall in this temperate climate is only 13 inches. Snowfall in higher elevations may accumulate into deep drifts and in areas may reach several feet.

When driving or hiking in Zion Canyon, or any of the park's higher elevations during winter or early spring, icy conditions should always

Below: A mantle of snow covers brush at midday in January with the Towers of the Virgin and the Beehives aglow in the background.
PHOTO BY TOM TILL

be of concern. Slippery trails and falling ice may be dangerous during winter. Hiking in canyons or the Narrows is not recommended as high runoff can lead to impassable areas and cold, fast moving water turning a fun hike into a life-threatening experience.

Chances are winter days will be surprisingly mild with cool nights. The many rewards of experiencing frozen waterfalls and ice crystal formations along Zion trails is well worth the effort as long as one uses prudence in selecting which trails to traverse and spends just a few minutes to check on conditions and safety regulations with the trained staff at the Visitor Center.

Snowmobiling, snowshoeing and cross-country skiing are available in Zion's higher elevations and at Cedar Breaks National Monument.

Left: Douglas fir cling to towering cliffs of Navajo sandstone in Zion National Park after a snowstorm.
PHOTO BY TOM DANIELSEN

Right: Yucca and ponderosa pines growing among Zion's massive cliffs of Navajo sandstone are dusted with snow after a winter storm.
PHOTO BY TOM DANIELSEN

Little evidence of Paleo-Indians has been found in Zion National Park and the surrounding area, although it is thought small bands followed grazing animals into the region during the Pleistocene Epoch, or Ice Age, at least 11,000 years ago.

As large game animals disappeared, due to climactic changes and pressure from hunters, plants, seeds and small game were sought by migratory hunter-gatherers who dominated the Southwest from around 3000 BC until the first century AD. It is likely this early culture found its way to areas near Zion, though there is little evidence to record their presence.

Around 500 AD, the Anasazi inhabited the Zion area although they did not construct the elaborate pueblos they are known for in the Four Corners region of the Southwest. They were skilled in weaving, pottery making and hunting with bows and arrows. They planted crops of corn, squash, beans and melons using sticks to make holes for seeds which were left to nature for water and nourishment. All that remains of their occupation of Zion are some pictographs– drawings painted on stone– and petroglyphs– drawings carved into stone, the remains of a few masonry granaries which were used to store food and the foundation of a single multi-roomed pueblo.

Around 1200 AD, the Anasazi withdrew from the region and the Paiutes began to settle. Semi-nomadic, they were basically hunter-gatherers although they farmed along streams and springs using irrigation and cultivation techniques learned from earlier contact with the Anasazi. The Paiutes lived in the area for several centuries, but were plagued by attacks from Navajos and Utes who ventured into the area and raided Paiute settlements.

In 1776, two Spanish missionaries, Fathers Escalante and Dominguez, and members of their expedition became the first Europeans to explore Utah. While searching for an overland route to connect missions in Monterey, California with those in Santa Fe, New Mexico they traveled within twenty miles of Zion but did not explore the area.

In 1826, mountain man Jedediah Smith became the first American to explore the region, traveling the Old Spanish Trail. Four years later, trapper George Yount traveled north of Zion en route to California. Traders, miners and trappers traveled the Old Spanish Trail, passing close to Zion between 1830 and 1850, but did not enter the area.

Mormons arrived in the region in 1858, when Nephi Johnson, a young Mormon missionary, was dispatched to the area under orders from Mormon leader Brigham Young. His mission was to convert the Indians and serve as an interpreter for the wagon trains of immigrants passing through the area. Nephi Johnson was lead by a group of Indians into Zion Canyon, which he explored in search of suitable farm land. It is unknown how far into the canyon he actually traveled. By some accounts he traveled as far as the Great White Throne, and by others, to the entrance to the Narrows.

Left: Pinnacles of the Court of the Patriarchs glow in the morning sun. The early Mormons exploring Zion Canyon had little time, or regard, for Indian names. In awe of towering features they beheld, they chose religious and inspirational names to describe Zion landmarks.
PHOTO BY TOM TILL

Right: Ruin of an Anasazi granary in an alcove above the Virgin River. The Anasazi occupied Zion between 500 AD and 1200 AD but did not construct the elaborate pueblos they are noted for in the Four Corners region.
PHOTO BY TOM TILL

THE ARRIVAL OF MAN CONTINUED...

The Mormons were interested in areas that were suitable for settlement of their rapidly growing membership and settled in nearby Toquerville and Virgin City in 1858. During the 1860s, hundreds of Mormon families began to settle the areas surrounding Zion. By 1861, crops were being raised and herds were being grazed in Zion Canyon.

St. George was settled as the capital of the territory in 1862 and was followed by settlements in Springdale, Rockville and Grafton. The Paiutes, who had for centuries been subject to Utes from the north– who demanded tribute and took Paiute children for slaves– and had been raided periodically by Navajos from the south, were no match for the iron will and manifest destiny of the Mormons. Today, the Paiutes, who numbered near 2000 in 1860, are few in number and are only found in scattered families in Cedar City, Parowan and Enterprise or on nearby reservations.

In 1871 and 1872, Major John Wesley Powell, the one-armed Civil War Veteran responsible for exploration of the Grand Canyon and much of the rest of the Colorado Plateau, sent members of his field survey party to explore Parunuweap Canyon and neighboring Zion Canyon, which Powell called Mukuntuweap (a Paiute name meaning "straight canyon."

Powell insisted on honoring Native American place names in his studies and later lobbied Congress to keep the name of Zion Mukuntuweap but was not to prevail as the feeling of the day was it was a difficult name to pronounce and meant little to white travelers. Photographs from the Powell survey party, by J.K. Hillers, of Angels Landing, Court of the Patriarchs and the Gate to Zion brought national attention to Zion.

In 1908, Leo A. Snow, deputy surveyor for the US government, surveyed the township that included Zion Canyon. His report extolling the beauty of Zion was so compelling that it was brought to the attention of President William Howard Taft (1857-1930) by the secretary of the interior with recommendations the area be declared a national monument. President Taft designated the area Mukuntuweap National Monument on July 31, 1909.

The Mukuntuweap name was changed to Zion in 1918, and the following year the area was designated Zion National Park. During the 1920s and 1930s road building– including the 5607 foot long Pine Creek Tunnel, truly a major engineering feat for its time– brought an easier public access to Zion.

Above: An Anasazi petroglyph of concentric circles, with an anthromorph next to it below an additional phosphene design, scratched into the surface of a Navajo sandstone wall.
PHOTO BY TOM DANIELSEN

Left: The Watchman looms over Zion National Park's south entrance monument. The monument and its original signs were constructed by the Civilian Conservation Corps, during the 1930s. The Civilian Conservation Corps, the brain child of President Franklin D. Roosevelt, was created to keep Americans working during the Great Depression when private sector jobs were scarce.
PHOTO BY TERRY DONNELLY

Right: Deciduous trees line the banks of the Virgin River on the Gateway to the Narrows Trail and show the greens and gold of early autumn.
PHOTO BY TERRY DONNELLY

Outside back cover: Brightly colored cottonwoods, *Populus Fremontii,* and the Navajo sandstone walls of the Temple of Sinawava in early fall in Zion Canyon, Zion National Park.
PHOTO BY TERRY DONNELLY